From the Pages of the *Tao Te Ching*

The Tao is so vast that when you use it, something is always left.

(chapter 4)

To hold until full is not as good as stopping.
An oversharpened sword cannot last long.
A room filled with gold and jewels cannot be protected.
Boasting of wealth and virtue brings your demise.
After finishing the work, withdraw.   (chapter 9)

Though you lose the body, you do not die.   (chapter 16)

Believe in the complete and return to it.   (chapter 22)

Know Glory but cleave to Humiliation
Be the valley for everyone.   (chapter 28)

What goes around comes around.   (chapter 30)

The Tao is always nameless.   (chapter 32)

True virtue does not "act"
And has no intentions.   (chapter 38)

Loss is not as bad as wanting more.   (chapter 46)

If I had just a little bit of wisdom
I should walk the Great Path and fear only straying from it.
Though the Way is quite broad
People love shortcuts.   (chapter 53)

One who knows does not speak.
One who speaks does not know. (chapter 56)

The Tao is hidden deeply in all things. (chapter 62)

Respond to anger with virtue.
Deal with difficulties while they are still easy.
Handle the great while it is still small. (chapter 63)

There is nothing better than to know that you don't know.
(chapter 71)

That the soft overcomes the hard
And the gentle overcomes the aggressive
Is something that everybody knows
But none can do themselves. (chapter 78)

True words are not fancy.
Fancy words are not true. (chapter 81)

The way of Heaven is to help and not harm. (chapter 81)

Tao Te Ching

Lao Tzu

With an Introduction and Notes by
YI-PING ONG

Translated by
CHARLES MULLER

GEORGE STADE
CONSULTING EDITORIAL DIRECTOR

BARNES & NOBLE CLASSICS
NEW YORK

ℬ
BARNES & NOBLE CLASSICS
NEW YORK

Published by Barnes & Noble Books
122 Fifth Avenue
New York, NY 10011

www.barnesandnoble.com/classics

The *Tao Te Ching* is thought by most modern scholars to have been written sometime between the late fourth century and early third century B.C. The present translation by Charles Muller was written in 1991 and revised in 1997.

Published in 2005 by Barnes & Noble Classics with new Introduction, Notes, Biography, Chronology, and For Further Reading.

Tao Te Ching
ISBN-13: 978-1-59308-256-7
ISBN-10: 1-59308-256-8
LC Control Number 2004112104

Produced and published in conjunction with:
Fine Creative Media, Inc.
322 Eighth Avenue
New York, NY 10001

Michael J. Fine, President and Publisher

Printed in the United States of America

QM

13   15   17   19   20   18   16   14   12

Lao Tzu

As with many ancient texts, controversy persists over when the *Tao Te Ching* was written, the details of its author's life, and whether the author is a true historical figure. Legend has it that Lao Tzu (the name means "Old Master") was born in the sixth century B.C. Carried in his mother's womb for seventy-two years, he entered the world with the white hair of an elderly man. In his first century B.C. biography of Lao Tzu, Ssu-ma Ch'ien reported legendary claims that Lao Tzu lived for more than 200 years.

According to Taoist tradition, Lao Tzu was a keeper of archives in the imperial court of the Zhou Dynasty (1027–221 B.C.). As a young man, Confucius sought information about propriety and rites, central concerns of Confucian morality, and he arranged an interview with the older Lao Tzu at court. Lao Tzu brilliantly instructed Confucius on the meaninglessness of his concerns. Following their meeting, Confucius compared Lao Tzu to a dragon in flight riding on the wind and clouds, invulnerable to the moral pitfalls that ensnare lesser men.

At the age of retirement, the legend goes, Lao Tzu, disillusioned with the state of the government, left his native territory and traveled west by water buffalo. At the border, a guard implored Lao Tzu to write down his teachings, and the result was the 5,000 words, or characters, of the *Tao Te Ching*. No more was heard from Lao Tzu after he passed through the border gates, and the date and place of his death remain unknown.

Some scholars claim that Lao Tzu was a name assigned to one of three men: Tan, prefect of the Grand Scribes; Lao Lai Tzu, an old Taoist sage; or the father of Tuan-kan Tsung, another historical person about whom not much is known. Another theory claims that a group of Taoist poets together wrote the *Tao Te Ching* and chose Lao Tzu as the author's name.

Table of Contents

The World of Lao Tzu and the *Tao Te Ching*

C. 2200–
1700 B.C.

According to tradition, the Xia Dynasty marks the beginning of imperial China. Legend holds that Yü, the Tamer of the Flood, drains the waters of a great deluge and makes China habitable. Yü makes rulership hereditary and creates the first imperial dynasty. Although the identity of the Xia civilization was long more legendary than firmly historical, late-twentieth-century archaeological work has confirmed its existence.

C. 1700–
1027

The Shang Dynasty, the first historic Chinese dynasty, comes into power, tradition says, after a rebel overturns the last ruler of the Xia Dynasty. The Shang capitals are alive with court life. The archaeological remains of one capital, located at the site of the modern city of Anyang, suggest a complex agricultural society that includes peasants, artisans, a priestly class, nobles, and a king. The first Chinese writing appears as inscriptions carved or brushed on tortoise shells and cattle bones (called "oracle bones"). Bronze work, which includes exquisite ceremonial vessels and weapons, reaches a pinnacle of development. The Shang Chinese worship their ancestors and make sacrifices to propitiate spirits.

1027–
771

The Western Zhou period of the Zhou Dynasty begins with the overthrow of the last Shang ruler. A political system founded on feudal city-states and a network of family connections helps maintain order and sustains the power of the kings. After some 200 years, barbarian tribes sack the imperial capital in 771 and kill the Zhou king. His son rises to power, and the capital moves eastward.

770   The Eastern Zhou Dynasty begins. During this dynasty's Spring and Autumn Period (770–476), the empire breaks into many small states that vie for power. A time of great change begins: Iron implements are introduced, crop yields increase as large irrigation projects are undertaken, and trade intensifies as the size and number of cities grow. The Chinese writing system develops. Despite the political disorder, the arts and culture flourish.

500s Based on a legendary account of a meeting between Lao Tzu and Confucius (see entry below), Lao Tzu lives and writes the *Tao Te Ching* (though modern scholars agree that the text likely appeared in the late fourth century or early third century). According to tradition, Lao Tzu is an archivist in the library of the Zhou Dynasty court. Later in his life he will leave the court and travel west on a water buffalo to reach the great desert. At the westernmost gate, a guard will demand that he write down his teachings, unrecorded until this point. The collected teachings become the *Tao Te Ching*.

551   Confucius is born in the small feudal state of Lu. A scholar in his youth, he becomes a great teacher whose ideas attract many followers. His philosophy is found in the *Analects*, the main collection of his sayings. According to legend, as a young man Confucius seeks information about propriety and rites and arranges a meeting with the older Lao Tzu at the imperial court. Lao Tzu brilliantly instructs him on the meaninglessness of these central concerns of Confucian morality.

479   Confucius dies, leaving behind many followers who spread his teachings of proper conduct and universal nobility.

475   The Warring States Period begins and will continue to

the end of the Zhou Dynasty in 221. Power is consolidated among fewer but stronger states that fight continually for control. Beginning with the late Spring and Autumn Period (see 770, above) and continuing through this one is the era known as the Hundred Schools of Thought, an intellectually creative time when the major Chinese philosophies—Taoism, Confucianism, Mohism, and Legalism—develop.

C.369   Chuang Tzu, considered one of the foremost early interpreters of Taoism, is born. His teachings are known as the *Chuang Tzu*.

221–   The Qin Dynasty begins when the western state of Qin
207   overpowers other states. The boundaries of the resulting state roughly match those of all subsequent dynasties.

C.145   Ssu-ma Ch'ien is born. He will write the *Shih Chi* (*Records of the Historian*), an influential history of China that includes legends of the life of Lao Tzu.

A.D. 440   Taoism becomes a state religion.

LATE 1700s Jesuit missionaries in China translate the *Tao Te Ching* into Latin. In the following centuries the work will be translated into numerous languages.

1868   John Chalmers translates the *Tao Te Ching* into English for the first time. The book will be translated into English more than forty times.

1973   Two copies of the *Tao Te Ching*, written on silk, are discovered in a tomb in Hunan province. Archaeologists learn that the burial date of the man in the tomb is 168 B.C. "Text A" and "Text B," as they are called, are not identical in style and content, and they spark a flurry of new scholarship and renewed debates over the origin and authorship of the work.

1993   The oldest copy of the *Tao Te Ching* discovered so far is found in a tomb in Guodian, in Hubei province. Dated

C. 300 B.C., the text survives intact despite the fragility of the bamboo strips on which it was written. Some scholars argue that this text provides evidence that the *Tao Te Ching* is the work of numerous authors and editors over many years.

Introduction

The *Tao Te Ching* is one of the most widely translated classics of all time and is without doubt the most widely translated work in Chinese. From East to West, generations of readers have marveled at its mystical yet simple profundity. It is considered to be the single most important text of Taoism. However, the question of how exactly it should be classified does not admit of a clear answer. Is the *Tao Te Ching* a book of ethics? Is it a religious text? Is it philosophical, especially given its focus on the deepest and truest way of seeing reality? Or is it, in fact, a work of literary genius—playful, poetic, paradoxical? No doubt the text has aspects of each and can be enjoyed for its poetry no less than for its reflections on human affairs, life, the universe, and the nature of the good. Nevertheless, one might wonder if there is an essential message to the *Tao Te Ching* and whether, as a consequence, there is a genre to which this message belongs.

Many have called it a book of wisdom, part of the so-called "wisdom tradition" that predates any single religion and that finds expression in texts as disparate as the *Bhagavad Gita*, the Socratic dialogues, and the biblical book of Proverbs. These works typically extol the study of both virtue and the obstacles to virtue; they attempt to reveal the path to right relations between humans, and to right relations between humans and the universe. Like the *Tao Te Ching*, these texts often focus on two primary methods by which one can acquire a deeper knowledge of virtue: gaining self-knowledge and rejecting worldly aims and standards. However, if the *Tao Te Ching* is to be thought of as a book of wisdom, what sense can be made of its attacks on wisdom and virtue? "Get rid of 'holiness' and abandon 'wisdom' and the people will benefit a hundredfold," it proclaims (chapter 19). And in another passage, on the incommensurability of the Tao and virtue, we are told: "True virtue is not virtuous / Therefore it has virtue. / Superficial virtue never fails to be virtuous / Therefore it has no virtue" (chapter 38).

Upon encountering passages such as these, even the most dedicated reader may feel a temptation to reinterpret or simplify away the ensuing confusion. However, before dismissing these paradoxes as senseless, or relegating them to the level of mere word play, we must go back to the beginning—the beginning of the text, that is. There we are told, "The Tao that can be followed is not the eternal Tao. / The name that can be named is not the eternal name" (chapter 1). The internal resistance of the text itself to categorization, especially as a work that attempts to teach the nature of virtue in a way that can be "named" or "followed," is no accident.

As with most texts that are as ancient as the *Tao Te Ching*, there remains some controversy over both the historical dating of the work and the biographical details of its author, Lao Tzu. The traditional view dates the text back to the sixth century B.C., largely on the basis of accounts describing a meeting between Confucius and Lao Tzu. These accounts describe Lao Tzu as an older man who is a contemporary of the younger Confucius (551–479 B.C.). However, reports of the supposed meeting were not accepted as tradition until the middle of the third century B.C., thus rendering their authority somewhat doubtful. Most modern scholars agree that the *Tao Te Ching* emerged in the late fourth century or early third century, about 2,500 years ago. In fact, stone tablets dated to around 300 B.C. have been found engraved with recognizable fragments of the text. Such a date would place the writing of the text at the height of one of the most intellectually productive times in Chinese history, known as the "Hundred Schools of Thought." During this time a multitude of philosophies were developed and a rich culture of intellectual debate flourished. Besides Taoism, other schools such as Confucianism, Legalism, and Mohism gave rise to the central classical texts that were to exert a great influence on Chinese thought over the next two millennia.

The name "Lao Tzu" was not the personal name of the author, but one bestowed upon him out of respect: "Lao" means "old" or "venerable," and "Tzu" is an honorific term attached to the names of scholars that can be roughly translated as "master." Very little was recorded about the actual life of Lao Tzu, and consequently there is much disagreement regarding his historical existence. Although he is mentioned on scrolls dating as far back as 400 B.C., many have attributed this appearance in the historical record to mere legend. Indeed, the legends surrounding the life of Lao Tzu are truly fantastic. The historian Ssu-ma Ch'ien, author of the *Shih Chi* (*Records of the Historian*), reports claims that Lao Tzu lived to more than two hundred years of age! Other legends maintain that he was born with white hair. According to Taoist tradition, he was an archivist who worked in the imperial library of the Zhou Dynasty court. It was there that he supposedly met Confucius, who had come to inquire about propriety and rites. Lao Tzu proceeded to dazzle him with his deep insight into the meaninglessness of these basic tenets of Confucian morality. According to this same story, Lao Tzu later resigned from his post in the Zhou court, then traveled west on a water buffalo to reach the great desert. He was stopped by a guard at the westernmost gate. This guard demanded that Lao Tzu—who had never, until this point, written down a word of his teachings—leave a record of his wisdom before he departed forever into the desert. The result of this request was the *Tao Te Ching*.

Legends aside, many scholars claim that "Lao Tzu" is actually a name attributed to at least one of three different men: Tan, Prefect of the Grand Scribes; Lao Lai Tzu, an old Taoist sage; or the father of Tuan-kan Tsung, another historical person about whom not much is known. Since the lifetimes of these three men span a range of a few hundred years, the lack of conclusive evidence either way suggests to some that Lao Tzu was none of these. According to another theory, the name "Lao Tzu" was chosen by a group of Taoist poets who actually composed the *Tao Te Ching* together. Wanting to shroud the composition of their text in a certain aura of mystery, they created a magical character without historical reality. A work by such an author would seem as if it were not of this world, and thus become even more appealing to readers.

The legend of the encounter between Lao Tzu and Confucius is one of the key pieces of evidence supporting Lao Tzu's existence; however, skepticism about its historical accuracy is supported by a consideration of the possible motives of the Taoists. Some scholars suggest that the Taoists may have crafted this story to demonstrate Lao Tzu's superior wisdom and undermine the authority of the Confucians. In fact, there were many popular stories invented by rivals of Confucius poking fun at him, such as one that "recalled" conversations between Confucius and a hermit in which the hermit was clearly much wiser than the great sage. The encounter between Lao Tzu and Confucius may just have been one of these stories. Not only would it have reflected well upon the Taoist school to have its main text authored by a sage capable of enlightening Confucius, the unearthly length of Lao Tzu's life and his mysterious disappearance into the west would no doubt have lent a certain credibility to his wisdom.

Even if this particular ploy on the part of the Taoists remains the mere conjecture of intellectual historians, competition between the Taoists and the Confucians is a verifiable fact. The two philosophies could not be more directly opposed to one another. Confucianism is primarily concerned with rites or propriety (*li*), a body of rules governing action in virtually every area of life. Of equal importance is the concept of righteousness (*i*), a transcendent standard by which the morality of these rules is to be evaluated. According to Confucius, one cultivates one's character by observing the rites scrupulously with the appropriate inner attitude of reverence. Because outward behavior can be superficial, Confucius claims that discerning knowledge about righteousness is necessary in order to distinguish mere rote observance of the rites from accordance with the true spirit of the rites.

The principal meaning of the rites is that they embody or express recognition of the value of human relations. Confucianism can be understood, in short, as a philosophy in which the social and ethical relations between people are of central importance. In the *Analects*, the main collection of Confucian sayings, both the observance of filial piety and the practice of benevolence (*jen*) are praised. Along with other virtues like honesty, courage, and loyalty, love and obligations to one's family members and others form the basis of the Confucian morality. Confucius also emphasizes the guidelines for the proper exercise of political power; as with the moral imperatives, these come from the "Decree of Heaven" (*t'ien ming*), the Heaven-approved mandate that gave rulers legitimacy as long as they were just. Rulers were to inspire good conduct and benevolence in their subjects not through punishment, but by example.

Critics of Confucian thought deplore its overemphasis on duty and hierarchy; they say that the many sayings and rites have a stultifying effect on the very people they are supposed to benefit. Rather than focusing on the human relations themselves, these critics argue, the elaborate system of practices established by Confucianism leads to rigidity and solidifies a social hierarchy. Such practices and the expectations that they produce lead some to feel superior to others, and make those who do not have the proper "cultivation" feel shameful and ignorant for no good reason.

Taoism can certainly be seen as a reaction against these undesirable aspects of Confucianism. Indeed, strands of the criticism voiced above are evident throughout the *Tao Te Ching*. While Confucius, with his active life of teaching and government advising, is the model Confucian sage who attempts to engage with the social and political world, Lao Tzu (whether real or fictitious) embodies a different ideal. Retiring from the struggle and corruption of the social realm to live in harmony with nature, Lao Tzu represents the Taoist conviction that the path of "action through inaction" (*wu-wei)* is the superior one.

The notion of *wu-wei* has been greatly misunderstood, no doubt because of its translation as "inaction" by previous generations of scholars. They interpreted it as a kind of passive quiescence; they depicted the Taoists as advocating an unthinking and essentially indolent approach to life. While it is true that the Taoists eschewed the activity of the political and social realm in favor of a more serene, contemplative way, it is not true that *wu-wei* can be thought of simply as inaction. The concept really refers to a kind of intuitive cooperation with the natural order, which is perfect and harmonious when left to work without the interference of ignorant human action. The idea that "action through inaction" is the most effective and least disruptive way of achieving one's goals is a central theme throughout the *Tao Te Ching*, one to which we will return.

If we contrast the Taoist notion of *wu-wei* with the Confucian emphasis on self-cultivation and adherence to the rites, it is evident why the Confucians could find Taoism to be rather threatening to their philosophy. As opposed to the safe, conventional order imposed by Confucian moral law, the Taoists believe in a kind of spontaneity that seems mystical and unreliable in comparison. Confucians claim that virtue is best learned when exemplified in rites, duties, and exemplary models; the Taoists argue that:

> When the Tao is lost there is virtue
> When virtue is lost there is *humaneness*
> When *humaneness* is lost there is rightness
> And when rightness is lost there is propriety.

> Now "propriety" is the external appearance of
> loyalty and sincerity
> And the beginning of disorder (chapter 38).

In associating the loss of the Tao with the achievement of the central aims of Confucian self-cultivation, the *Tao Te Ching* not only diverges from the central moral concepts of the Confucian worldview—it places itself in clear opposition to the very foundation upon which these concepts are based.

The Taoist alternative to the rules and customs of the social world is depicted by its critics as a kind of mystic contemplation, a practice that favors the liberty of the individual at the expense of his or her duties and relationships. This extreme individualism is held to be highly problematic by other schools of thought. From the more grounded perspective of Confucian and Legalist philosophies, Taoism seems nihilistic and dangerous. It endangers the cohesive social fabric that the rules and laws of the other philosophies seek to create. The Taoist teaching that a simple merging with the Tao is far superior to any mastery of complicated moral teachings appears to justify a kind of ignorant amorality, with no verifiable standards or criteria. Furthermore, the Taoist belief that the best government does not try to exert any influence upon its subjects stands in direct contradiction to the Confucian model of the ruler as moral paragon. Passages such as these from the *Tao Te Ching* go so far as to express blatant support for a kind of anarchy: "The reason the river and sea can be regarded as / The rulers of all the valley streams / Is because of their being below them. / . . . If you want to lead [people] / You must place yourself behind them" (chapter 66). The idea of a political state that did not legitimize the authority and power of the ruler over the subjects was intolerable to adherents of other philosophies.

Another important dispute between the Confucian and Taoist schools concerns the "rectification of names" (*cheng-ming*), which Confucius teaches is essential to establishing right relationships. The "rectification of names" entails knowing and fixing a reliable association between a name and the thing to which it properly refers. Of particular importance are those names that inform people of their place in the social hierarchy, and of the way in which they should behave. Thus, a king should be called a "king" only if he acts like one; the same would hold true for a father, a son, and others. Since accurate naming plays such a vital role in guiding ethical conduct, Confucius argues in the *Analects* that *cheng-ming* was the first thing that must be established if one wanted to administer a government well.

In contrast, the *Tao Te Ching* indicates that the Taoists hold a much more ambivalent view about language. In this text, words and concepts are not considered to be one of the ways in which one can understand or gain access to the mystery of the Tao. The Tao is essentially nameless, undifferentiated, and lacking in form. The order and rules of language, if they have any function at all, have the potential to corrupt the natural harmony of the universe. The following passage reveals how skepticism about the power of naming is linked to a pointed questioning of the Confucian model of political authority:

> The Tao is always nameless.
> And even though a sapling might be small
> No one can make it be his subject.
> If rulers could embody this principle
> The myriad things would follow on their own.
> Heaven and Earth would be in perfect accord
> And rain sweet dew.
>
> People, unable to deal with It on its own terms
> Make adjustments;
> And so you have the beginning of division into names.
> Since there are already plenty of names
> You should know where to stop.
> Knowing where to stop, you can avoid danger (chapter 32).

At the beginning of the passage, the namelessness of the Tao is associated with the absence of any ruling hierarchy. The way in which the Tao is devoid of any conceptual or legal order should reflect the peace and harmony of the sociopolitical world, which would be assured by the absence of any hierarchy that names like "king" and "subject" inevitably impose. Humans, however, are prone to grasp for power and status, and are therefore unable to deal with the radical lack of distinctions inherent in the nature of the Tao. This human ignorance is manifested in "the beginning of division into names," which the author implies might lead to some kind of "danger."

How are we to understand the nature of this danger? There is first of all the danger of not understanding the Tao on its own terms, and introducing misleading divisions as if they reflected something about reality. Another way of explaining this point is in terms of the danger inherent in dualistic thinking. The human mind has a tendency to divide the world into opposites: black and white, good and bad, beautiful and ugly, night and day. In reality, "night" can only be understood as "night" in relation to "day." There is no such thing as "night" without "day," in the sense that we could not even *conceive* of the idea of "night" without also having a concept of "day." The pairs of concepts are convenient ways for us to designate relative differences. However, an overly rigid dualism can obscure the true nature of reality. Without understanding that "night" and "day" are only so in relation to one another, I might start to think that "night" actually refers to some essential entity that exists in and of itself without the presence of "day." Similarly, if I think that something is *good* in and of itself and another thing is *bad*, I will be motivated to pursue the good and destroy the bad. Not realizing that the good does not exist without the bad, my judgment becomes a kind of prejudice that arouses an adversarial relationship to things in the world. That is why the *Tao Te Ching* declares, "Get rid of 'learning' and there will be no anxiety. / How much difference is there between 'yes' and 'no' ? / How far removed from each other are 'good' and 'evil' ?" (chapter 20).

Conceptual dichotomies can make the mind rigid, oriented toward one thing and away from another. The desire and aversion that arise create anxiety. This message underlies another seemingly paradoxical passage from the *Tao Te Ching*: "All in the world recognize the beautiful as beautiful. / Herein lies ugliness. / All recognize the good as good. / Herein lies evil" (chapter 2). Recognizing some quality or something as essentially beautiful, one is not able to see its deeper nature, that which goes beyond its conventional characterization as "beautiful" or "not ugly." Think of medicine, which we ordinarily consider to be beneficial and healing. Even the best medicine, when taken in excess, can kill someone. In a similar way, we might think of human waste as bad. But without it we could not rid the body of toxins or fertilize the soil for future cultivation. This way of considering the ambivalent nature of things is not, however, how we normally think. We like to divide the world up into good things (medicine, food, wealth, friends, etc.) and bad things (waste, dirt, emptiness, enemies, etc.), no matter how simplistic this might be. Our ignorance fosters greed and striving for the "good," as well as hatred and fear of the "evil." Such states of mind and the actions that result are "ugly" and "evil," in so far as they prevent us from understanding the natural harmony and wholeness that already exist in the Tao.

In contrast to a perspective informed by absolute dichotomies, the *Tao Te Ching* teaches the nature of interdependence. Opposites are related to one another; indeed, they arise from one another:

> Being and non-being produce each other.
> Difficulty and ease bring about each other.
> Long and short delimit each other.
> High and low rest on each other.
> Sound and voice harmonize each other.
> Front and back follow each other (chapter 2).

An understanding of the profound relationship between seemingly disparate things is developed concurrently with the practice of *wu-wei*. If one is not striving for the good or against the bad, then there is no isolated aim at which one's action is directed. It is the lack of a dualistically established aim that renders one's action "without action" and in accordance with the deeper, non-dualistic nature of the Tao. Within the Tao, opposites exist without contradicting or competing against one another. Each is recognized to be necessary for the other.

According to the *Tao Te Ching*, not only can reliance on the names and categories of language lead to a distorted view of reality, it can also create misunderstanding about what is truly beneficial. Unity and oneness with the Tao are destroyed when one believes that people belong to separate roles and have different moral standings. Thus

Lao Tzu says, "When your constancy in virtue is complete / You return to the state of the 'uncarved block.' / The block is cut into implements. / The sage uses them to fulfill roles. / Therefore the great tailor does not cut" (chapter 28). The uncarved block, an image of a stone without any writing or distinguishing marks on it, represents a mind that is one with the undifferentiated Tao. The sage who cuts up reality in order to devise some kind of order, purpose, and functionality in the social and natural realm ("to fulfill roles") breaks the unity and purity of the intact block. He is trying to achieve something that already exists in a state of perfection, without any human intervention.

Such a worldview is very far from the Confucian notion of virtue, in which recognizable paragons, standards, and hierarchies constitute the structure in which moral character and behavior can be learned. People are considered to be virtuous in so far as they fulfill their proper roles and functions. To Lao Tzu, however, even the distinction between virtuous and immoral can only lead to destructive ambitions, as people vie to become better than others. "If you do not adulate the worthy, you will make others non-contentious" (chapter 3). It is wiser not to follow human laws, because in following the Tao one becomes humble and aware of the underlying unity of all things.

Although some people interpret the *Tao Te Ching* as being totally relativistic in its perspective on reality, we can see that this is not the case. The relativism in the *Tao Te Ching*, if it can even be thought of as relativism, is presented as an antidote to the dogmatic way in which language and social hierarchy are used in other schools of thought. An overemphasis on learning, cultivation, and social position can keep one from seeing the perfection of the natural order and the needlessness of striving. Therefore, a certain kind of moral and intellectual exertion is seen as a deviation from the original peacefulness. Naive relativism declares that "anything goes," but this is not the view expressed in the *Tao Te Ching*. Rather, the dogmatic insistence that one way is better than another way is rejected because it does not allow one to attain the purity of an existence in harmony with the Tao. It is only in contrast, then, with the position of other philosophies that Taoism can be considered to be anarchic, nihilistic, or relativistic. Taken on its own terms, it clearly advocates a certain path or way of life that is portrayed as being more faithful to reality: "Human beings follow the Earth. / Earth follows Heaven / Heaven follows the Tao / The Tao follows the way things are" (chapter 25).

In understanding this path, it has been most useful to start with what it is *not*. Now we may ask, what *is* the Tao? This is a difficult question, in part because the Tao is principally characterized in terms of its ineffability. "Existing continuously, it cannot be named and it returns to no-thingness" (chapter 14). When it is given a more definitive characteristic, the concepts that are associated with it nevertheless stretch the limits of language and imagination: It is called eternal, nameless, and perfect:

> There is something that is perfect in its disorder
> Which is born before Heaven and Earth. . . .
> We can regard it as the Mother of Everything.
>
> I don't know its name.
>
> Hence, when forced to name it, I call it "Tao."
> When forced to categorize it, I call it "great" (chapter 25).

In this passage, the author declares that the choice of "Tao" for the nameless "Mother of Everything" is made merely for the conventional purpose of naming; the reader should not get caught up in trying to discover the nature of the "Tao" from its name. However, the selection of "Tao" as a name is not without significance. The concept of Tao, or "the Way," is an ancient one that predates both Confucian and Taoist schools of thought. Even Confucius said, "He has not lived in vain who dies the day he is told about the Way" (*Analects*, chapter 4, verse 8). The word "Tao," when used in this context, designates the deepest nature of reality or truth. Thus "Tao" is not a concept unique to Taoism, but one that is used to mean different things according to different schools of thought.

In the *Tao Te Ching*, this ultimate truth or Way is distinctly conceived of as one that is transcendent and beyond the reach of human minds. This is not to say that it cannot be understood at all. It can be observed and partly grasped in many ways, but it can never be grasped completely by any individual mind or encompassed in the finite meaning of any concept. The idea that the ultimate Tao cannot be captured is what underlies the opening passage of the *Tao Te Ching*: "The Tao that can be followed is not the eternal Tao. / The name that can be named is not the eternal name. / The nameless is the origin of heaven and earth / While naming is the origin of the myriad things" (chapter 1). Those who claim to know the Way, who claim to be able to categorize it relative to other named entities, are ignorant of its true greatness. They are mistaking some lesser thing for the Tao, and thus their attempts to realize the truth will be frustrated and futile.

The namelessness of the Tao obviously complicates any attempt of the author to make reference to it. Thus the language of paradox and nothingness in the *Tao Te Ching* is introduced not as a definitive way of categorizing the Tao, but as a way of showing what it is not. Images of absence and emptiness, for example, indicate that the common mind is so engaged with what is there that it ignores the very important reality of what is not there:

> Thirty spokes join together in the hub.
> It is because of what is not there that the cart is useful.
> Clay is formed into a vessel.
> It is because of its emptiness that the vessel is useful.
> Cut doors and windows to make a room.
> It is because of its emptiness that the room is useful.
> Therefore, what is present is used for profit.
>
> But it is in absence that there is usefulness (chapter 11).

Like the empty space within a room that allows for life-giving air, the emptiness of the Tao is able to give rise to and sustain the myriad forms of existence. Although its emptiness does not allow it to be sold or valued as conventionally existent things are, it is in fact this non-being that provides the condition for the existence of all other things.

In addition to such imagery, the author of the *Tao Te Ching* also uses paradox as a device to lead the reader directly to a realization of the Tao. Consider a passage such as the following, which ostensibly describes the Tao: "Thus, it is called the formless form, / The image of no-thing. / This is called the most obscure" (chapter 14). Such a description confounds the attempt of the mind to grasp it, either by abstract thought or concrete visualization. When one tries to call to mind the "image of no-thing" or conceive of a form without form, one is struck by the impossibility of it. Paradox stuns the mind of the reader and stymies any attempt to analyze or comprehend the Tao by conventional thought. When the processes of the intellect have effectively been paralyzed, one's intuition becomes free to enter into the Tao without the frustration of trying to grasp it conceptually.

Although there are many passages thick with the language of paradox, much of the imagery in the *Tao Te Ching* is also direct and simple. "To speak little," Lao Tzu tells us, "is natural" (chapter 23). Thus he often seeks to explain the principles of the Tao by using straightforward examples, without making reference to complex, abstract ideas. Taoism is not, after all, an esoteric school of thought; it is intended to address the very heart of ordinary concerns, such as the protection of life and peace of mind. Its truths are evident in the most basic and natural phenomena: the movement of water, the growth of plants, the plain facts of human nature, and other obvious aspects of the world. Although these matters may appear mundane, the wisdom of the Tao is revealed when one examines them closely.

What could be more simple or intuitive than the facts of life and death? What is more fundamental to all beings than the desire to survive? If we think carefully about what leads to life and what sustains life, we can understand something about the Tao:

When people are born they are gentle and soft.
At death they are hard and stiff.
When plants are alive they are soft and delicate.
When they die, they wither and dry up.
Therefore the hard and stiff are followers of death.
The gentle and soft are the followers of life.

Thus, if you are aggressive and stiff, you won't win.
When a tree is hard enough, it is cut. Therefore
The hard and big are lesser,
The gentle and soft are greater (chapter 76).

Life and its preservation depend on the qualities of being "gentle and soft." In order to be aware of the changes in one's environment, one must be sensitive and in touch with one's vulnerability. In order to go along with these changes, one must also be supple and flexible enough to adapt. That is why it is said: "The gentle and soft overcomes the hard and aggressive. / A fish cannot leave the water" (chapter 36). In the end, accepting one's dependence on the delicate balance of nature is more important than striving to gain mastery over the world.

Furthermore, being "gentle and soft" also protects one by helping one to go unnoticed by those who are foolish enough to live according to the spirit of competition. Those who are competitive seek one another out and attempt to vie with each other, since they are grasping for power and control. Being "aggressive and stiff" naturally makes one a target for destruction by such people. The *Tao Te Ching* makes a point of noting how this principle has a clear application to human affairs:

The best warrior is never aggressive.
The best fighter is never angry.
The best tactician does not engage the enemy.
The best utilizer of people's talents places himself below them.

This is called the virtue of non-contention.

It is called the ability to engage people's talents.

It is called the ultimate in merging with Heaven (chapter 68).

The purpose of being a warrior, fighter, or tactician is to survive longer than one's enemy. The aim of all political arts is the preservation of life. Even power is simply a means to this end, without which nothing would matter. The way to survive is not to seek war or provoke others, but to be peaceful and humble. In this way, one avoids engaging in a struggle that will eventually lead to death. A skillful warrior or politician who tries to rule over others with power and glory only invites the envy of others, whose hatred provides a motivation for the development of a greater power. The cycle of domination and killing is endless, unless we develop the wisdom not to begin it.

The "virtue of non-contention" is what leads the *Tao Te Ching* to declare that "If you used the Tao as a principle for ruling / You would not dominate the people by military force" (chapter 30). Passages such as this one have led some to interpret Taoism as favoring weakness over strength, passivity over activism, and surrender over boldness. However, this interpretation is misleading, for what seems "weak" actually triumphs over what is "strong." Force always has a brittle quality: It stands against something, and hence creates an opposition to itself. The character of force makes it susceptible and weaker than what is flexible, accommodating, and gentle. Thus compassion is considered to be stronger than aggression: "If you wage war with compassion you will win. / If you protect yourself with compassion you will be impervious" (chapter 67).

The analogy from nature evoked to illustrate this point is the wearing away of stone by water. "Nothing in the world is softer than water, / Yet nothing is better at overcoming the hard and strong. / This is because nothing can alter it" (chapter 78). Water is the most yielding element there is—softer than flesh, softer than rock, it evaporates in the heat of the sun and seems to be contained within the confines of the soil. But its flexibility allows it to regenerate in the form of rain; its patience allows it to wear away even the largest, most dense stone. Being yielding, it never has to change its essence. It remains utterly pure. It is also considered to be the life force, for without water, everything would dry up and die. For all of these reasons, water is considered to give us insight into the nature of the Tao. "The highest goodness is like water. / Water easily benefits all things without struggle. / Yet it abides in places that men hate. / Therefore it is like the Tao" (chapter 8).

Like the Tao itself, the subjects of plants and water, life and death, and war and peace are simple and easy to understand, while simultaneously being rich in many meanings. The use of metaphor thus allows the author to make deeper philosophical points about the superiority of Taoism without engaging the rhetoric and arguments of other schools. For example, a passage in the *Tao Te Ching* draws our attention to the way in which simple and humble things give rise to what is great: "A thick tree grows from a tiny seed. / A tall building arises from a mound of earth. / A journey of a thousand miles starts with one step. / Contriving, you are defeated; / Grasping, you lose" (chapter 64). The obvious message of this passage is that if we try to complicate our lives, developing clever plans and ambitions, we lose sight of the way in which small, insignificant things actually hold the key to what we seek. Even an effortless action can lead to "a journey of a thousand miles." In the same way, however, the passage makes another subtle point. The great mystery of the Tao can be understood only through observing tiny and seemingly inconsequential things, and living simply. One who tries to study the complicated nuances of culture and morality will actually lose the Way and be "defeated" by her own unnecessary effort.

This, as we have seen, is a recurring theme in the *Tao Te Ching*. Whatever we think is valuable—power, wealth, wisdom—cannot be attained by trying to grasp it. The text reveals several ways of contemplating this single point:

In studying, each day something is gained.
In following the Tao, each day something is lost.
Lost and again lost.
Until there is nothing left to do.
Not-doing, nothing is left undone.
You can possess the world by never manipulating it.
No matter how much you manipulate
You can never possess the world (chapter 48).

We are invited to think about what happens when we think that we must do something to achieve or possess something else. We must start from the assumption that doing that thing will bring us something that we do not yet have. It is the nature of purposive action to arise from some sense of lack, some feeling of incompleteness. Following the Tao, one realizes that the intolerance of what is not leads to unhappiness. Action is meaningless, because the pursuit of gain leads us only to become more convinced of our own inadequacy or the imperfection of the world as it is.

This is one of the strangest paradoxes for the student of the Tao to grasp. The more one understands of the Tao, the less one knows. With its simple message, spare prose, and natural imagery, the *Tao Te Ching* itself provides an example of *wu-wei*. It attains an effortless wisdom, a kind of understanding without understanding: a philosophy that embodies its own message. One does not become a follower of the Tao by studying or knowing it. "Truth," we are told, "seems contradictory" (chapter 78).

Yi-Ping Ong graduated *summa cum laude* in 1999 from Columbia University, with a major in philosophy and a minor in east Asian languages and cultures. She went on to read philosophy and theology at Oxford, where she also studied Sanskrit and Mahayana Buddhist ethics, graduating in 2001. She is currently completing a Ph.D. in philosophy at Harvard University with a focus on moral and political philosophy. In 2002 she led a workshop on human rights in Asia at the

Harvard Project for Asia and International Affairs conference in Sydney. She has worked and traveled throughout Japan, India, and Cambodia, and serves as the director of a volunteer program for a nongovernmental organization in rural India. Her fiction has been published in the *Harvard Review*.

Tao Te Ching

壹篇

The Tao that can be
followed is not the
eternal Tao

1

The Tao that can be followed is not the eternal Tao.
The name that can be named is not the eternal name.
The nameless is the origin of heaven and earth
While naming is the origin of the myriad things.
Therefore, always desireless, you see the mystery
Ever desiring, you see the manifestations.[1]
These two are the same—
When they appear they are named differently.

This sameness is the mystery,
Mystery within mystery;

The door to all marvels.

貳篇

All in the world recog-
nize the beautiful as
beautiful

2

All in the world recognize the beautiful as beautiful.
Herein lies ugliness.
All recognize the good as good.
Herein lies evil.

Therefore
Being and non-being produce each other.
Difficulty and ease bring about each other.
Long and short delimit each other.
High and low rest on each other.
Sound and voice harmonize each other.
Front and back follow each other.

Therefore the sage abides in the condition of *wu-wei*
    (unattached action).
And carries out the wordless teaching.
Here, the myriad things are made, yet not separated.

Therefore the sage produces without possessing,
Acts without expectations
And accomplishes without abiding in her
    accomplishments.[2]

It is precisely because she does not abide in them
That they never leave her.[3]

叁篇

If you do not adulate the worthy . . .

3

If you do not adulate the worthy, you will make others
    non-contentious.
If you do not value rare treasures, you will stop others
    from stealing.
If people do not see desirables, they will not be agitated.

Therefore, when the sage governs,
He clears people's minds,
Fills their bellies,
Weakens their ambition and
Strengthens their bones.

If the people are kept without cleverness and desire
It will make the intellectuals not dare to meddle.

Acting without contrivance, there is no lack of
    manageability.

肆 篇

The Tao is so vast . . .

4

The Tao is so vast that when you use it, something is
    always left.
How deep it is!
It seems to be the ancestor of the myriad things.
It blunts sharpness
Untangles knots
Softens the glare
Unifies with the mundane.
It is so full!
It seems to have remainder.

It is the child of I-don't-know-who.
And prior to the primeval Lord-on-high.[4]

伍篇

Heaven and Earth are not humane . . .

5

Heaven and Earth are not humane,[5]
And regard the people as straw dogs.[6]
The sage is not humane,
And regards all things as straw dogs.
The space between Heaven and Earth is just like a
    bellows:
Empty it, it is not exhausted.
Squeeze it and more comes out.

Investigating it with a lot of talk
Is not like holding to the center.

陸篇

The valley spirit never
dies . . .

6

The valley spirit never dies.
It is called "the mysterious female."
The opening of the mysterious female
Is called "the root of Heaven and Earth."[7]
Continuous, seeming to remain.

Use it without exertion.

柒篇

Heaven and Earth last forever . . .

7

Heaven and Earth last forever.
The reason that Heaven and Earth are able to last forever
Is because they do not give birth to themselves.
Therefore, they are always alive.
Hence, the sage puts herself last and is first.
She is outside herself and therefore her self lasts.

Is it not through her selflessness
That she is able to perfect herself?

捌篇

The highest goodness is
like water . . .

8

The highest goodness is like water.
Water easily benefits all things without struggle.
Yet it abides in places that men hate.
Therefore it is like the Tao.

For dwelling, the Earth is good.
For the mind, depth is good.
The goodness of giving is in the timing.
The goodness of speech is in honesty.
In government, self-mastery is good.
In handling affairs, ability is good.

If you do not wrangle, you will not be blamed.

玖 篇

To hold until full is not
as good as stopping . . .

9

To hold until full is not as good as stopping.
An oversharpened sword cannot last long.
A room filled with gold and jewels cannot be protected.
Boasting of wealth and virtue brings your demise.
After finishing the work, withdraw.

This is the Way of Heaven.

拾篇

Pacifying the agitated material soul . . .

10

Pacifying the agitated material soul and holding to
   oneness:
Are you able to avoid separation?
Focusing your energy on the release of tension:
Can you be like an infant?
In purifying your insight:
Can you un-obstruct it?
Loving the people and ruling the state:
Can you avoid over-manipulation?
In opening and closing the gate of Heaven:
Can you be the female?[8]
In illuminating the whole universe:
Can you be free of rationality?

Give birth to it and nourish it.
Produce it but don't possess it.
Act without expectation.
Excel, but don't take charge.

This is called Mysterious Virtue.

壹拾壹篇

Thirty spokes join together in the hub . . .

11

Thirty spokes join together in the hub.
It is because of what is not there that the cart is useful.
Clay is formed into a vessel.
It is because of its emptiness that the vessel is useful.
Cut doors and windows to make a room.
It is because of its emptiness that the room is useful.
Therefore, what is present is used for profit.

But it is in absence that there is usefulness.

壹拾貳篇

The five colors blind our eyes . . .

12

The five colors blind our eyes.
The five tones deafen our ears.
The five flavors confuse our taste.
Racing and hunting madden our minds.

Possessing rare treasures brings about harmful behavior.
Therefore the sage regards his center, and not his eyes.

He lets go of that and chooses this.

壹拾叁篇

Accept humiliation as a surprise . . .

13

Accept humiliation as a surprise.
Value great misfortune as your own self.

What do I mean by "Accept humiliation as a surprise"?
When you are humble
Attainment is a surprise
And so is loss.
That's why I say, "Accept humiliation as a surprise."

What do I mean by "Value great misfortune as your own
   self"?

If I have no self, how could I experience misfortune?

Therefore, if you dedicate your life for the benefit of the
   world,
You can rely on the world.
If you love dedicating yourself in this way,
You can be entrusted with the world.

壹拾肆篇

Look for it, it cannot be
seen . . .

14

Look for it, it cannot be seen.
It is called the distant.
Listen for it, it cannot be heard.
It is called the rare.
Reach for it, it cannot be gotten.
It is called the subtle.
These three ultimately cannot be fathomed.
Therefore they join to become one.

Its top is not bright;
Its bottom is not dark;
Existing continuously, it cannot be named and it returns
    to no-thingness.

Thus, it is called the formless form,
The image of no-thing.
This is called the most obscure.

Go to meet it, you cannot see its face.
Follow it, you cannot see its back.

By holding to the ancient Tao
You can manage present existence
And know the primordial beginning.

This is called the very beginning thread of the Tao.

壹拾伍篇

The ancient masters of
the Tao . . .

15

The ancient masters of the Tao
Had subtle marvelous mystic penetration
A depth that cannot be known.
It is exactly because they are unknowable

That we are forced to pay attention to their appearance.
Hesitant, like one crossing an ice-covered river.
Ready, like one afraid of his neighbors on all sides.
Dignified, like a guest.
Loose, like ice about to melt.
Straightforward, like an uncarved block of wood.
Open, like a valley.
Obscure, like muddy water.

Who can be muddled, and use clarity to gradually
    become lucid?
Who can be calm, and use constant application for
    eventual success?

The one who holds to this path does not crave
    fulfillment.
Precisely because he does not crave fulfillment
He can be shattered
And do without quick restitution.

壹拾陸篇

Effect emptiness to the extreme . . .

16

Effect emptiness to the extreme.
Keep stillness whole.
Myriad things act in concert.
I therefore watch their return.
All things flourish and each returns to its root.

Returning to the root is called quietude.
Quietude is called returning to life.
Return to life is called constant.
Knowing this constant is called illumination.
Acting arbitrarily without knowing the constant is
    harmful.
Knowing the constant is receptivity, which is impartial.

Impartiality is kingship.
Kingship is Heaven.
Heaven is Tao
Tao is eternal.

Though you lose the body, you do not die.[9]

壹拾柒篇

From great antiquity forth
they have known and
possessed it . . .

17

From great antiquity forth they have known and
    possessed it.
Those of the next level loved and praised it.
The next were in awe of it.
And the next despised it.[10]

If you lack sincerity no one will believe you.

How careful she is with her precious words!
When her work is complete and her job is finished,
Everybody says: "We did it!"

壹拾捌篇

When the great Tao
perishes . . .

18

When the great Tao perishes
There is *humaneness* and rightness.
When intelligence is manifest
There is great deception.
When the six relationships are not in harmony[11]
There is filial piety and compassion.
When the country is in chaos
Loyal ministers appear.

壹 拾 玖 篇

Get rid of "holiness" . . .

19

Get rid of "holiness" and abandon "wisdom" and the
people will benefit a hundredfold.

Get rid of "humaneness" and abandon "rightness" and
the people will return to filial piety and
compassion.[12]

Get rid of cleverness and abandon profit, and thieves
and gangsters will not exist.

Since the above three are merely words, they are not
sufficient.
Therefore there must be something to include them all.

See the origin and keep the non-differentiated state.
Lessen selfishness and decrease desire.

貳拾篇

Get rid of "learning" . . .

20

Get rid of "learning" and there will be no anxiety.
How much difference is there between "yes" and "no"?
How far removed from each other are "good" and "evil"?
Yet what the people are in awe of cannot be disregarded.

I am scattered, never having been in a comfortable center.
All the people enjoy themselves, as if they are at the
    festival of the great sacrifice,[13]
Or climbing the Spring Platform.[14]
I alone remain, not yet having shown myself.
Like an infant who has not yet laughed.

Weary, like one despairing of no home to return to.

All the people enjoy extra
While I have left everything behind.
I am ignorant of the minds of others.
So dull!
While average people are clear and bright, I alone am
    obscure.
Average people know everything.
To me alone all seems covered.
So flat!
Like the ocean.
Blowing around!
It seems there is no place to rest.
Everybody has a goal in mind.
I alone am as ignorant as a bumpkin.
I alone differ from people.

I enjoy being nourished by the mother.

貳拾壹篇

The form of great

virtue . . .

21

The form of great virtue is something that only the Tao
    can follow.
The Tao as a "thing" is only vague and obscure.
How obscure! How vague! In it there is form.
How vague! How obscure! In it are things.
How deep! How dark! In it there is an essence.

The essence is so real—therein is belief.[15]

From the present to antiquity, its name has never left it,
    so we can examine all origins.
How do I know the form of all origins?

By this.

貳 拾 貳 篇

The imperfect is completed . . .

22

The imperfect is completed.
The crooked is straightened.
The empty is filled.
The old is renewed.
With few there is attainment.
With much there is confusion.
Therefore the sage grasps the one and becomes the
    model for all.

She does not show herself, and therefore is apparent.
She does not affirm herself, and therefore is
    acknowledged.
She does not boast and therefore has merit.
She does not strive and is therefore successful.
It is exactly because she does not contend, that nobody
    can contend with her.

How could the ancient saying, "The imperfect is
    completed" be regarded as empty talk?

Believe in the complete and return to it.

貳拾叁篇

To speak little is natural . . .

23

To speak little is natural.
Therefore a gale does not blow a whole morning
Nor does a downpour last a whole day.

Who does these things? Heaven and Earth.
If even Heaven and Earth cannot force perfect continuity
How can people expect to?

Therefore there is such a thing as aligning one's actions
    with the Tao.
If you accord with the Tao you become one with it.
If you accord with virtue you become one with it.
If you accord with loss you become one with it.

The Tao accepts this accordance gladly.
Virtue accepts this accordance gladly.
Loss also accepts accordance gladly.

If you are untrustworthy, people will not trust you.

贰拾肆篇

Standing on tiptoe, you
are unsteady . . .

24

Standing on tiptoe, you are unsteady.
Straddle-legged, you cannot go.
If you show yourself, you will not be seen.
If you affirm yourself, you will not shine.
If you boast, you will have no merit.
If you promote yourself, you will have no success.

Those who abide in the Tao call these

Leftover food and wasted action
And all things dislike them.

Therefore the person of the Tao does not act like this.

貳拾伍篇

There is something that
is perfect in its
disorder . . .

25

There is something that is perfect in its disorder
Which is born before Heaven and Earth.

So silent and desolate! It establishes itself without
    renewal.
Functions universally without lapse.
We can regard it as the Mother of Everything.

I don't know its name.

Hence, when forced to name it, I call it "Tao."
When forced to categorize it, I call it "great."

Greatness entails transcendence.
Transcendence entails going-far.
Going-far entails return.

Hence, Tao is great, Heaven is great, the Earth is great
And the human is also great.

Within our realm there are four greatnesses and the
    human being is one of them.

Human beings follow the Earth.
Earth follows Heaven
Heaven follows the Tao
The Tao follows the way things are.

貳拾陸篇

Heaviness is the root of lightness . . .

26

Heaviness is the root of lightness.
Composure is the ruler of instability.
Therefore the sage travels all day
Without putting down his heavy load.
Though there may be spectacles to see
He easily passes them by.

This being so
How could the ruler of a large state
Be so concerned with himself as to ignore the people?

If you take them lightly you will lose your roots.
If you are unstable, you will lose your rulership.

貳 拾 柒 篇

A good traveler leaves
no tracks . . .

27

A good traveler leaves no tracks.
Good speech lacks faultfinding.
A good counter needs no calculator.
A well-shut door will stay closed without a latch.
Skillful fastening will stay tied without knots.[16]

It is in this manner that the sage is always skillful in
    elevating people.
Therefore she does not discard anybody.

She is always skillful in helping things
Therefore she does not discard anything.
This is called "the actualization of her luminosity."

Hence, the good are the teachers of the not-so-good.
And the not-so-good are the charges of the good.

Not valuing your teacher or not loving your students:
Even if you are smart, you are gravely in error.

This is called Essential Subtlety.

貳 拾 捌 篇

Know the Masculine,
cleave to the Feminine . . .

28

Know the Masculine, cleave to the Feminine
Be the valley for everyone.
Being the valley for everyone
You are always in virtue without lapse
And you return to infancy.

Know the White, cleave to the Black
Be a model for everyone.
Being the model for everyone
You are always in virtue and free from error
You return to limitlessness.
Know Glory but cleave to Humiliation
Be the valley for everyone.
When your constancy in virtue is complete
You return to the state of the "uncarved block."

The block is cut into implements.[17]
The sage uses them to fulfill roles.

Therefore the great tailor does not cut.

貳 拾 玖 篇

If you want to grab the
world and run it . . .

29

If you want to grab the world and run it
I can see that you will not succeed.
The world is a spiritual vessel, which can't be controlled.

Manipulators mess things up.
Grabbers lose it. Therefore:

Sometimes you lead
Sometimes you follow
Sometimes you are stifled
Sometimes you breathe easy
Sometimes you are strong
Sometimes you are weak
Sometimes you destroy
And sometimes you are destroyed.

Hence, the sage shuns excess
Shuns grandiosity
Shuns arrogance.

叁拾篇

If you used the Tao as a
principle for ruling . . .

30

If you used the Tao as a principle for ruling
You would not dominate the people by military force.

What goes around comes around.

Where the general has camped
Thorns and brambles grow.
In the wake of a great army
Come years of famine.
If you know what you are doing
You will do what is necessary and stop there.

Accomplish but don't boast
Accomplish without show
Accomplish without arrogance
Accomplish without grabbing
Accomplish without forcing.

When things flourish they decline.

This is called non-Tao
The non-Tao is short-lived.

叁拾壹篇

Sharp weapons are
inauspicious
instruments . . .

31

Sharp weapons are inauspicious instruments.
Everyone hates them.
Therefore the man of the Tao is not comfortable with
    them.

In the domestic affairs of the gentleman
The left is the position of honor.
In military affairs the right is the position of honor.[18]

Since weapons are inauspicious instruments, they are
    not the instruments of the gentleman
So he uses them without enjoyment
And values plainness.

Victory is never sweet.

Those for whom victory is sweet
Are those who enjoy killing.
If you enjoy killing, you cannot gain the trust of the
    people.

On auspicious occasions the place of honor is on the left.
On inauspicious occasions the place of honor is on the
    right.
The lieutenant commander stands on the left.
The commander-in-chief stands on the right.
And they speak, using the funerary rites to bury them.

The common people, from whom all the dead have come
Weep in lamentation.
The victors bury them with funerary rites.

叁拾贰篇

The Tao is always
nameless . . .

32

The Tao is always nameless.
And even though a sapling might be small
No one can make it be his subject.
If rulers could embody this principle
The myriad things would follow on their own.
Heaven and Earth would be in perfect accord
And rain sweet dew.

People, unable to deal with It on its own terms
Make adjustments;
And so you have the beginning of division into names.
Since there are already plenty of names
You should know where to stop.
Knowing where to stop, you can avoid danger.

The Tao's existence in the world

Is like valley streams running into the rivers and seas.

叁 拾 叁 篇

If you understand others
you are smart . . .

33

If you understand others you are smart.
If you understand yourself you are illuminated.
If you overcome others you are powerful.
If you overcome yourself you have strength.
If you know how to be satisfied you are rich.
If you can act with vigor, you have a will.
If you don't lose your objectives you can be long-lasting.

If you die without loss, you are eternal.

叄拾肆篇

The Tao is like a great
flooding river . . .

34

The Tao is like a great flooding river. How can it be
    directed to the left or right?
The myriad things rely on it for their life but do not
    distinguish it.
It brings to completion but cannot be said to exist.

It clothes and feeds all things without lording over them.

It is always desireless, so we call it "the small."
The myriad things return to it and it doesn't exact
    lordship
Thus it can be called "great."
Till the end, it does not regard itself as Great.

Therefore it actualizes its greatness.

叁 拾 伍 篇

Holding to the Great Form . . .

35

Holding to the Great Form
All pass away.
They pass away unharmed, resting in Great Peace.

It is for food and music that the passing traveler stops.

When the Tao appears from its opening
It is so subtle, it has no taste.
Look at it, you cannot see it.
Listen, you cannot hear it.
Use it

You cannot exhaust it.

叁 拾 陸 篇

That which will be
shrunk . . .

36

That which will be shrunk
Must first be stretched.
That which will be weakened
Must first be strengthened.
That which will be torn down
Must first be raised up.
That which will be taken
Must first be given.

This is called "subtle illumination."

The gentle and soft overcomes the hard and aggressive.

A fish cannot leave the water.

The country's potent weapons
Should not be shown to its people.

叁拾柒篇

The Tao is always "not-doing" . . .

37

The Tao is always "not-doing"
Yet there is nothing it doesn't do.
If the ruler is able to embody it
Everything will naturally change.

Being changed, they desire to act.

So I must restrain them, using the nameless "uncarved
    block (original mind)."

Using the nameless uncarved block
They become desireless.
Desireless, they are tranquil and
All-under-Heaven is naturally settled.

叁 拾 捌 篇

True virtue is not virtuous . . .

38

True virtue is not virtuous[19]
Therefore it has virtue.
Superficial virtue never fails to be virtuous
Therefore it has no virtue.

True virtue does not "act"
And has no intentions.
Superficial virtue "acts"
And always has intentions.
True *humaneness* "acts"
But has no intentions.
True rightness "acts"
But has intentions.
True propriety "acts" and if you don't respond

They will roll up their sleeves and threaten you.

Thus, when the Tao is lost there is virtue
When virtue is lost there is *humaneness*
When *humaneness* is lost there is rightness
And when rightness is lost there is propriety.

Now "propriety" is the external appearance of loyalty
    and sincerity
And the beginning of disorder.

Occult abilities are just flowers of the Tao[20]
And the beginning of foolishness.

Therefore the Master dwells in the substantial
And not in the superficial.
Rests in the fruit and not in the flower.

So let go of that and grasp this.

叁 拾 玖 篇

These in the past have
attained wholeness . . .

39

These in the past have attained wholeness:

Heaven attains wholeness with its clarity;
The Earth attains wholeness with its firmness;
The Spirit attains wholeness with its transcendence;
The Valley attains wholeness when filled;
The Myriad Things attain wholeness in life;
The Ruler attains wholeness in the correct governance
    of the people.

In effecting this:
If Heaven lacked clarity it would be divided;
If the Earth lacked firmness it would fly away;
If the spirit lacked transcendence it would be exhausted;
If the valley lacked fullness it would be depleted;
If the myriad things lacked life they would vanish.
If the ruler lacks nobility and loftiness he will be
    tripped up.

Hence
Nobility has lowliness as its root
The High has the Low as its base.

Thus the kings call themselves "the orphan, the lowly,
    the unworthy."

Is this not taking lowliness as the fundamental? Isn't it?

In this way you can bring about great effect without
    burden.
Not desiring the rarity of gems
Or the manyness of grains of sand.

肆拾篇

Return is the motion of the Tao . . .

40

Return is the motion of the Tao.
Softening is its function.[21]
All things in the cosmos arise from being.
Being arises from non-being.

肆拾壹篇

When superior students hear of the Tao . . .

41

When superior students hear of the Tao
They strive to practice it.
When middling students hear of the Tao
They sometimes keep it and sometimes lose it.
When inferior students hear of the Tao
They have a big laugh.

But "not laughing" in itself is not sufficient to be called
the Tao, and therefore it is said:

The sparkling Tao seems dark
Advancing in the Tao seems like regression.
Settling into the Tao seems rough.

True virtue is like a valley.
The immaculate seems humble.
Extensive virtue seems insufficient.
Established virtue seems deceptive.
The face of reality seems to change.
The great square has no corners.
Great ability takes a long time to perfect.
Great sound is hard to hear.
The great form has no shape.

The Tao is hidden and nameless.

This is exactly why the Tao is good at developing and
perfecting.

肆拾貳篇

The Tao produces one, one produces two . . .

42

The Tao produces one, one produces two.
The two produce the three and the three produce all
    things.
All things submit to *yin* and embrace *yang*.
They soften their energy to achieve harmony.

People hate to think of themselves as "orphan," "lowly,"
    and "unworthy"
Yet the kings call themselves by these names.

Some lose and yet gain,
Others gain and yet lose.
That which is taught by the people
I also teach:
"The forceful do not choose their place of death."
I regard this as the father of all teachings.[22]

肆拾叁篇

The softest thing in the world . . .

43

The softest thing in the world
Will overcome the hardest.
Non-being can enter where there is no space.
Therefore I know the benefit of unattached action.[23]
The wordless teaching and unattached action

Are rarely seen.

肆拾肆篇

Which is dearer, fame or your life?

44

Which is dearer, fame or your life?
Which is greater, your life or possessions?
Which is more painful, gain or loss?
Therefore we always pay a great price for excessive love
And suffer deep loss for great accumulation.
Knowing what is enough, you will not be humiliated.
Knowing where to stop, you will not be imperiled

And can be long-lasting.

肆拾伍篇

Great perfection seems flawed . . .

45

Great perfection seems flawed, yet functions without a
    hitch.
Great fullness seems empty, yet functions without
    exhaustion.
Great straightness seems crooked,
Great skill seems clumsy,
Great eloquence seems stammering.

Excitement overcomes cold, stillness overcomes heat.[24]
Clarity and stillness set everything right.

肆拾陸篇

When the Tao prevails
in the land . . .

46

When the Tao prevails in the land
The horses leisurely graze and fertilize the ground.
When the Tao is lacking in the land
War horses are bred outside the city.
Natural disasters are not as bad as not knowing what is
    enough.
Loss is not as bad as wanting more.

Therefore the sufficiency that comes from knowing
    what is enough is an eternal sufficiency.

肆 拾 柒 篇

Without going out the door, knowing everything . . .

47

Without going out the door, knowing everything,
Without peaking out the windowshades, seeing the Way
of Heaven.

The further you go, the less you know.

The sage understands without having to go through the
whole process.
She is famous without showing herself.
Is perfected without striving.

肆 拾 捌 篇

In studying, each day
something is gained . . .

48

In studying, each day something is gained.
In following the Tao, each day something is lost.
Lost and again lost.
Until there is nothing left to do.
Not-doing, nothing is left undone.
You can possess the world by never manipulating it.
No matter how much you manipulate
You can never possess the world.

肆拾玖篇

The sage has no fixed mind . . .

49

The sage has no fixed mind,
She takes the mind of the people as her mind.

I treat the good as good, I also treat the evil as good.
This is true goodness.
I trust the trustworthy, I also trust the untrustworthy.
This is real trust.

When the sage lives with people, she harmonizes with
    them
And conceals her mind for them.
The sages treat them as their little children.[25]

伍拾篇

Coming into life and entering death . . .

50

Coming into life and entering death,
The followers of life are three in ten.
The followers of death are three in ten.
Those whose life activity is their death ground are three
    in ten.
Why is this?
Because they live life grasping for its rich taste.

Now I have heard that those who are expert in handling
    life
Can travel the land without meeting tigers and rhinos,
Can enter battle without being wounded.
The rhino has no place to plant its horn,
The tiger has no place to place its claws,
Weapons find no place to receive their sharp edges.
Why?

Because he has no death-ground.[26]

伍 拾 壹 篇

Tao gives birth to it . . .

51

Tao gives birth to it,
Virtue rears it,
Materiality shapes it,
Activity perfects it.
Therefore, there are none of the myriad things who do
    not venerate the Tao or esteem its virtue.
This veneration of the Tao and esteeming of its virtue is
    something they do naturally, without being forced.
Therefore, Tao gives birth.
Its virtue rears, develops, raises, adjusts and disciplines,

Nourishes, covers and protects,
Produces but does not possess,
Acts without expectation,
Leads without forcing.

This is called "Mysterious Virtue."

伍拾貳篇

All things have a
beginning, which we can
regard as their Mother . . .

52

All things have a beginning, which we can regard as
   their Mother.
Knowing the mother, we can know its children.
Knowing the children, yet still cleaving to the mother
You can die without pain.

Stop up the holes
Shut the doors,[27]
You can finish your life without anxiety.

Open the doors,
Increase your involvements,
In the end you can't be helped.

Seeing the subtle is called illumination.
Keeping flexible is called strength.
Use the illumination, but return to the light.
Don't bring harm to yourself.

This is called "practicing the eternal."

伍拾叁篇

If I had just a little bit of wisdom . . .

53

If I had just a little bit of wisdom
I should walk the Great Path and fear only straying from
    it.
Though the Way is quite broad
People love shortcuts.

The court is immaculate,
While the fields are overgrown with weeds,
And the granaries are empty.
They wear silk finery,
Carry sharp swords,
Sate themselves on food and drink
Having wealth in excess.
They are called thieving braggarts.

This is definitely not the Way.

伍 拾 肆 篇

The well-established
cannot be uprooted . . .

54

The well-established cannot be uprooted.
The well-grasped does not slip away.
Generation after generation carries out the ancestor
　　worship without break.

Cultivate it in yourself and virtue will be real.
Cultivate it in the family and virtue will overflow.
Cultivate it in the town and virtue will be great.
Cultivate it in the country and virtue will be abundant.
Cultivate it in the world and virtue will be everywhere.

Therefore, take yourself and observe yourself.
Take the family and observe the family.
Take the town and observe the town.
Take the country and observe the country.
Take the world and observe the world.

How do I know the world as it is?

By this.

伍拾伍篇

One who remains rich
in virtuous power . . .

55

One who remains rich in virtuous power
Is like a newborn baby.[28]
Bees, scorpions and venomous snakes do not bite it,
The wild beasts do not attack it,
Birds of prey do not sink their claws into it.
Though its bones are weak
And muscles soft,
Its grip is strong.
Without knowing of the blending of male and female
S/he is a perfect production,
The ultimate in vitality.
S/he cries all day without getting hoarse.
S/he is the ultimate in harmony.

Understanding harmony is called the Constant.
Knowing the Constant is called illumination.
Nourishing life is called blessing.
Having control of your breath is called strength.[29]

After things blossom they decay, and
This is called the non-Tao.

The non-Tao expires quickly.

伍拾陸篇

One who knows does
not speak . . .

56

One who knows does not speak.
One who speaks does not know.
Close your holes, shut your doors,
Soften your sharpness, loosen your knots.
Soften your glare and merge with the everyday.

This is called mysteriously attaining oneness.

Though you cannot possess it, you are intimate with it
And at the same time, distant.
Though you cannot possess it, you are benefitted by it,
And harmed by it.
You cannot possess it, but are esteemed through it
And humbled by it.

Therefore the world values you.

伍 拾 柒 篇

Use fairness in
governing the state . . .

57

Use fairness in governing the state.
Use surprise tactics in war.

Be unconcerned and you will have the world.
How do I know it is like this?
Because:
The more regulations there are,
The poorer people become.
The more people own lethal weapons,
The more darkened are the country and clans.
The more clever the people are,
The more extraordinary actions they take.
The more picky the laws are,
The more thieves and gangsters there are.

Therefore the sages say:

> I do not force my way and the people transform
>   themselves.
> I enjoy my serenity and the people correct
>   themselves.
> I do not interfere and the people enrich themselves.

> I have no desires

> And the people find their original mind.

伍 拾 捌 篇

When the government is laid back . . .

58

When the government is laid back
The people are relaxed.
When the government is nitpicking
The people have anxiety.
Misfortune depends upon fortune.
Fortune conceals misfortune.
What has a definite delimitation?
Or abnormality?

The normal reverts to strangeness.
Goodness reverts to perversion.

People certainly have been confused for a long time.

Therefore the sage squares things without cutting.
Edges without separating.
Straightens without lining up.

Shines but does not glare.

伍 拾 玖 篇

In governing the country
and serving Heaven . . .

59

In governing the country and serving Heaven
There is nothing like frugality.
Only by being frugal can you recover quickly.
When you recover quickly you accumulate virtue.
Having accumulated virtue,
There is nothing you can't overcome.
When there is nothing you can't overcome
Who knows the limits of your capabilities?
These limits being unfathomable
You can possess the country.

The Mother who possesses the country can be long-
    living.
This is called "planting the roots deeply and firmly."

The way to long life and eternal vision.

陸拾篇

Ruling a large country is like cooking a small fish . . .

60

Ruling a large country is like cooking a small fish.[30]
When you govern people with the Tao
Demons will have no power.
Not that they don't have power,
But their power will not harm people.

Since the sage doesn't harm people,
The two will not harm each other.

Here their power merges and returns.

陸拾壹篇

The great state should be like a river basin . . .

61

The great state should be like a river basin.
The mixing place of the world,
The feminine of the world.
The feminine always overcomes the masculine by
    softness
Because softness is lesser.
Therefore if a large state serves a small state
It will gain the small state.
If a small state serves a large state
It will gain the large state.

Therefore some serve in order to gain
And some gain despite their servitude.

The large state wants nothing more
Than to unite and feed its people.
The small state wants nothing more
Than to enter into the service of the right person.
Thus both get what they want.

Greatness lies in placing oneself below.

陸拾貳篇

The Tao is hidden deeply in all things . . .

62

The Tao is hidden deeply in all things.
It is the treasure of the good
And the refuge of the not-so-good.
With skillful words you can be successful.
With honorable actions you can be included.

People may not be so good, but how can you deny
    them?

Therefore, even though there are great jewels brought
    in by teams of horses at the coronation of the
    emperor and the installation of the three princes,
This is not as good as staying where you are
And advancing in this Tao.

Why did the ancients so value the Tao?

You can't say that it was for seeking gain
Or to have punishments to deter crime.

Therefore it is the most prized in the world.

陸拾叁篇

Do without "doing" . . .

63

Do without "doing."
Get involved without manipulating.
Taste without tasting.
Make the great small,
The many, few.
Respond to anger with virtue.[31]
Deal with difficulties while they are still easy.
Handle the great while it is still small.

The difficult problems in life
Always start off being simple.
Great affairs always start off being small.
Therefore the sage never deals with the great
And is able to actualize his greatness.

Now light words generate little belief,
Much ease turns into much difficulty.
Therefore the sage treats things as though they were
    difficult,

And hence, never has difficulty.

陸拾肆篇

That which is at rest is easy to grasp . . .

64

That which is at rest is easy to grasp.
That which has not yet come about is easy to plan for.
That which is fragile is easily broken.
That which is minute is easily scattered.
Handle things before they arise.
Manage affairs before they are in a mess.

A thick tree grows from a tiny seed.
A tall building arises from a mound of earth.
A journey of a thousand miles starts with one step.
Contriving, you are defeated;
Grasping, you lose.

The sage doesn't contrive, so she isn't beaten.
Not grasping, she doesn't lose.
When people are carrying out their projects
They usually blow it at the end.

If you are as careful at the end
As you were at the beginning,
You won't be disappointed.

Therefore the sage desires non-desire,
Does not value rare goods,
Studies the unlearnable
So that she can correct the mistakes of average people
And aid all things in manifesting their true nature

Without presuming to take the initiative.

陸拾伍篇

The ancients who were skillful at the Tao . . .

65

The ancients who were skillful at the Tao
Did not illuminate the people
But rather kept them simple.
When the people are difficult to rule

It is because of their cleverness.
Therefore
If you use cleverness to rule the state
You are a robber of the state.
If you don't use cleverness to rule the state
You are a blessing to the state.

If you understand these two points, you know the
    proper norm for governing.
To be continuously understanding the proper norm is
    called Mysterious Virtue.
How deep and far-reaching Mysterious Virtue is!
It makes all return

Until they reach the Great Norm.

陸 拾 陸 篇

The reason the river and
sea can be regarded
as . . .

66

The reason the river and sea can be regarded as
The rulers of all the valley streams
Is because of their being below them.
Therefore they can be their rulers.
So if you want to be over people
You must speak humbly to them.
If you want to lead them
You must place yourself behind them.

Thus the sage is positioned above
And the people do not feel oppressed.
He is in front and they feel nothing wrong.
Therefore they like to push him front and never resent
    him.

Since he does not contend

No one can contend with him.

陸拾柒篇

The reason everybody calls my Tao great . . .

67

The reason everybody calls my Tao great
Is because there is nothing quite like it.
It is exactly because it *is* great
That there is nothing quite like it.
If there were something that were consistently like it

How could it be small?

I have three treasures that I hold and cherish.
The first is compassion,
The second is frugality,
The third is not daring to put myself ahead of
    everybody.

Having compassion, I can be brave.
Having frugality, I can be generous.
Not daring to put myself ahead of everybody
I can take the time to perfect my abilities.
Now if I am brave without compassion
Generous without frugality, or
Go to the fore without putting my own concerns last,
I might as well be dead.

If you wage war with compassion you will win.
If you protect yourself with compassion you will be
    impervious.

Heaven will take care of you,

Protecting you with compassion.

陸拾捌篇

The best warrior is never aggressive . . .

68

The best warrior is never aggressive.
The best fighter is never angry.
The best tactician does not engage the enemy.
The best utilizer of people's talents places himself below
   them.

This is called the virtue of non-contention.
It is called the ability to engage people's talents.
It is called the ultimate in merging with Heaven.

陸拾玖篇

Strategists have a saying . . .

69

Strategists have a saying:
> I prefer to be able to move, rather than be in a fixed
> position
> I prefer to retreat a foot rather than advancing an
> inch.

This is called progress without advancing;
Preparing without showing off;
Smashing where there is no defense;
Taking him without a fight.

There is no greater danger than under-estimating your
opponent.
If I under-estimate my opponent
I will lose that which is most dear.
Therefore

When opponents clash

The one who is sorry about it will be the winner.[32]

柒拾篇

My words are easy to understand . . .

70

My words are easy to understand
And easy to practice.
Yet nobody understands them or practices them.
My words have an origin;
My actions have a principle.
It is only because of your not understanding this
That you do not understand me.
Since there are few who understand me
I am valued.
Therefore the sage wears coarse clothes.
Yet hides a jewel in his bosom.

柒拾壹篇

There is nothing better
than to know that you
don't know . . .

71

There is nothing better than to know that you don't
   know.
Not knowing, yet thinking you know—
This is sickness.
Only when you are sick of being sick
Can you be cured.
The sage's not being sick

Is because she is sick of sickness.

Therefore she is not sick.

柒拾貳篇

When the people do not fear your might . . .

72

When the people do not fear your might
Then your might has truly become great.
Don't interfere with their household affairs.
Don't oppress their livelihood.

If you don't oppress them they won't feel oppressed.

Thus the sage understands herself
But does not show herself.
Loves herself
But does not prize herself.
Therefore she lets go of that

And takes this.

柒拾叁篇

If you are courageous in
daring you will die . . .

73

If you are courageous in daring you will die.
If you are courageous in not-daring you will live.
Among these two, one is beneficial and the other is
    harmful.

Who understands the reason why Heaven dislikes what
    it dislikes?
Even the sage has difficulty in knowing this.

The Way of Heaven is to win easily without struggle.

To respond well without words,
To naturally come without special invitation,
To plan well without anxiety.

Heaven's net is vast.
It is loose.

Yet nothing slips through.

柒拾肆篇

If the people don't fear death . . .

74

If the people don't fear death
How will you scare them with death?
If you make the people continuously fear death
By seizing anybody who does something out of the
    ordinary
And killing them,
Who will dare to move?

There is always an official executioner to handle this.
If you play the role of the official executioner
It is like cutting wood in the capacity of Master
    Carpenter.

There are few who will not cut their hands.

柒拾伍篇

The reason people

starve . . .

75

The reason people starve
Is because their rulers tax them excessively.
They are difficult to govern

Because their rulers have their own ends in mind.

The reason people take death lightly
Is because they want life to be rich.
Therefore they take death lightly.
It is only by not living for your own ends
That you can go beyond valuing life.

柒拾陸篇

When people are born
they are gentle and
soft . . .

76

When people are born they are gentle and soft.
At death they are hard and stiff.
When plants are alive they are soft and delicate.
When they die, they wither and dry up.
Therefore the hard and stiff are followers of death.
The gentle and soft are the followers of life.

Thus, if you are aggressive and stiff, you won't win.
When a tree is hard enough, it is cut. Therefore
The hard and big are lesser,
The gentle and soft are greater.

柒拾柒篇

The Way of Heaven . . .

77

The Way of Heaven
Is like stretching a bow.[33]
The top is pulled down,
The bottom is pulled up.
Excess string is removed
Where more is needed, it is added.

It is the Way of Heaven
To remove where there is excess
And add where there is lack.
The way of people is different:
They take away where there is need
And add where there is surplus.

Who can take his surplus and give it to the people?
Only one who possesses the Tao.

Therefore the sage acts without expectation.
Does not abide in his accomplishments.
Does not want to show his virtue.

柒 拾 捌 篇

Nothing in the world is
softer than water . . .

78

Nothing in the world is softer than water,
Yet nothing is better at overcoming the hard and strong.
This is because nothing can alter it.

That the soft overcomes the hard
And the gentle overcomes the aggressive
Is something that everybody knows
But none can do themselves.
Therefore the sages say:

> The one who accepts the dirt of the state
> Becomes its master.
> The one who accepts its calamity
> Becomes king of the world.

Truth seems contradictory.

柒拾玖篇

After calming great
anger . . .

79

After calming great anger
There are always resentments left over.
How can this be considered as goodness?
Therefore the sage keeps her part of the deal
And doesn't check up on the other person.

Thus virtuous officials keep their promise
And the crooked ones break it.

The Heavenly Tao has no favorites:

It raises up the Good.

捌 拾 篇

Let there be a small
country with few
people . . .

80

Let there be a small country with few people,
Who, even having much machinery, don't use it.
Who take death seriously and don't wander far away.
Even though they have boats and carriages, they never
    ride in them.
Having armor and weapons, they never go to war.
Let them return to measurement by tying knots in
    rope.[34]

Sweeten their food, give them nice clothes, a peaceful
    abode and a relaxed life.

Even though the next country can be seen and its dogs
    and chickens can be heard,

The people will grow old and die without visiting each
    other's land.

捌拾壹篇

True words are not fancy . . .

81

True words are not fancy.
Fancy words are not true.
The good do not debate.
Debaters are not good.
The one who really knows is not broadly learned,
The extensively learned do not really know.
The sage does not hoard,
She gives people her surplus.
Giving her surplus to others she is enriched.

The way of Heaven is to help and not harm.

Endnotes

1. (chapter 1) *Ever desiring, you see the manifestations*: Desire aims at definite objects or states of affairs. When we see the world through the lens of desire, reality becomes fractured into what we want and what we do not want. When we desire, our hearts and minds are oriented toward the world "of the myriad things." When we are without desire, however, we see the "mystery" of the Tao that resides beyond its various manifestations. Similarly, naming is said to give rise to multiplicity, because most names refer to particular, finite things. Giving something a name sets it apart from other things. The Tao is therefore characterized as nameless, because it is without finite form.

2. (chapter 2) *And accomplishes without abiding in her accomplishments*: The sage is one who "produces without possessing" because she realizes that things arise of their own accord, and not as the result of her own coercion or anxious striving. She is not the one who brings things about, and so she does not feel any sense of ownership over the result of her actions. That is why *wu-wei* can be translated as "unattached action." To act in a way that shows an attachment to the action is to have a definite aim in mind, to be frustrated if things do not happen according to one's expectations, and to congratulate oneself for one's effort if things do happen in the "right" way. She who understands *wu-wei* does not hold this view of her actions.

3. (chapter 2) *That they never leave her*: The feminine pronoun is used deliberately to refer to the Taoist sage. Taoism is unique among the major schools of Chinese thought in emphasizing the priority of the feminine principle (*yin*) over the masculine principle (*yang*). *Yin* and *yang* have been considered since ancient times to be the two opposing forces or principles of the universe.

Confucianism can be said to privilege the masculine principle, which is associated with a world of formal language, laws, activity, and the desire to control and master nature. In contrast, the feminine principle is creative, life-giving, yielding, intuitive, and compassionate. Throughout the *Tao Te Ching*, the characterization of the Tao reveals that it has many qualities that may be thought of as *yin*. The text also emphasizes that the dominance of qualities associated with *yang* can obstruct one's access to, and understanding of, the Tao. "The feminine always overcomes the masculine by softness" (chapter 61).

4. (chapter 4) *And prior to the primeval Lord-on-high*: The "Lord-on-High" refers to God, or the first ancestor.

5. (chapter 5) *Heaven and Earth are not humane*: The word that is translated as "humane" here is *jen*, the Confucian virtue of benevolence. See the Introduction for an explanation of the philosophical disagreement between Taoism and Confucianism on the value of moral concepts devised by people.

6. (chapter 5) *And regard the people as straw dogs*: Chapter 14 of the *Chuang Tzu*, the work of the important Taoist philosopher Chuang Tzu, describes how straw dogs were treated very respectfully before being presented for sacrifice, and afterward were trampled on and swept away. All things are to be destroyed after they have served their purpose.

7. (chapter 6) *Is called "the root of Heaven and Earth"*: The "valley spirit" refers to the Tao. A valley is a fertile place, reminiscent of a womb that gives birth to and nourishes all beings. Hence the Tao is also called "the mysterious female," because it is the origin of Heaven and Earth. It is said to be "continuous" in the sense that it is immortal and gives rise to beings without ceasing. One cannot exhaust its creative force.

8. (chapter 10) *In opening and closing the gate of Heaven: Can you be the female?*: "Opening and closing the gate of Heaven" has been interpreted variously by scholars. Some think that "the gate of Heaven" refers to the five senses, which reveal the world to us.

Some think that it refers to the act of inhaling and exhaling, and may be an allusion to esoteric Taoist yogic practices. According to a passage from the *I-Ching* (*Book of Changes*), an ancient Chinese divination manual and book of wisdom, it signifies the alternation between the Creative and Receptive forces and thus refers to the creation and sustaining of the universe. Being "the female" may be understood in contrast to those aspects of the masculine principle that are undesirable—ruling over creation, trying to establish one's own power and control, and being possessive over what one thinks one has made. "The female" nurtures the world but does not "over-manipulate" it or "take charge" of it. This is the "Mysterious Virtue," the ability to create without glorying in the exercise of one's own power.

9. (chapter 16) *Though you lose the body, you do not die*: The possibility of immortality alluded to here can be interpreted in many ways. Taken in context with the rest of the passage, the deathlessness of the self could refer to the way in which one becomes eternal by forgetting one's finite self and merging with the transcendent reality of the Tao. Upon losing one's identification with the body, one returns to the source of all life. Certain Taoist meditative practices may also have been thought to help one's soul survive the process of death and attain immortality. The process of "returning to the root" refers to the way in which consciousness becomes still and finds its way back to the original emptiness that is prior to all thought and form. The Tao returns individuated life forms to their primeval source.

10. (chapter 17) *From great antiquity forth they have known and possessed it. / . . . And the next despised it*: This four-line passage refers to the four levels of government, from the most to the least desirable. The most desirable is that which is just known, neither loved nor feared, and so unobtrusive that its works are one with the activities of everyone.

11. (chapter 18) *When the six relationships are not in harmony*: The six

relations are father-son, elder brother-younger brother, and husband-wife.

12. (chapter 19) *Get rid of "humaneness" and abandon "rightness" and the people will return to filial piety and compassion*: "Humaneness" (*jen*) and "rightness" (*i*) refer to the moral virtues advocated by Confucianism.

13. (chapter 20) *All the people enjoy themselves, as if they are at the festival of the great sacrifice*: "The festival of the great sacrifice" refers to a banquet at which three animals—the cow, the sheep, and the pig—are eaten.

14. (chapter 20) *Or climbing the Spring Platform*: This probably refers to a sightseeing platform.

15. (chapter 21) *The essence is so real—therein is belief*: The character translated here as "essence" (*ching*) can mean also spirit, life force, life seed, or vitality. The character translated as "belief" (*hsin*) can also mean evidence, proof, truth, sincerity, or faith. The "essence" within the Tao is the life seed, or beginning of things. Yet the life force, or potential, in the Tao is so real and so actual that it contains within it the certainty or proof of its being.

16. (chapter 27) *Skillful fastening will stay tied without knots*: In this passage, goodness is associated with not leaving a trace. The Tao is ineffable; that which follows in the way of the Tao imitates its essential subtlety. Three lines above, "Good speech lacks faultfinding," for example, because it is not calculating and does not seek to establish marked differences. Relative differences do exist, but they should not be made into absolute differences as justification for "discard[ing]" what is considered to be bad. As the passage goes on to declare, "the good are the teachers of the not-so-good. / And the not-so-good are the charges of the good." The virtuous serve as models for the "not-so-good," but they actually need those people who are "not-so-good"—otherwise they would have no one for whom to be exemplary! "Essential Subtlety" entails such an awareness of the interdependence of opposites.

17. (chapter 28) *The block is cut into implements*: This metaphor alludes

to the way in which the original integrity of human nature is shaped and cultivated to fit different roles in society, in particular those official functions developed by governments to serve a specialized purpose.

18. (chapter 31) *In military affairs the right is the position of honor*: As the passage goes on to state, "On auspicious occasions the place of honor is on the left. / On inauspicious occasions the place of honor is on the right." At ceremonies celebrating the joys and triumphs of life, the left is honored; at ceremonies marking loss and grief, the right is honored. The death and destruction following war clearly mark it as inauspicious, an occasion for deep mourning over the loss of life. In following the Tao, one realizes that destroying life can never be understood as a victory.

19. (chapter 38) *True virtue is not virtuous . . . .* : Traditionally, the *Tao Te Ching* was divided into two books known as the "Tao Classic" and the "Te Classic." This chapter is the first chapter of the second book. The name of the book comes from the principal subject of this chapter: "*Te*," which means power or virtue. For more on the contrast between the Taoist and Confucian interpretations of virtue, see the introduction.

20. (chapter 38) *Occult abilities are just flowers of the Tao*: "Occult abilities," such as fortune telling and the art of divination, are mere ornaments that distract one from the deeper reality of the Tao.

21. (chapter 40) *Return is the motion of the Tao. / Softening is its function*: The notion of "return" is fundamental to an understanding of the Tao. Of the Tao itself, it is said, "Existing continuously, it cannot be named and it returns to no-thingness" (chapter 14). The "myriad things" are described as going back to their source: "All things flourish and each returns to its root" (chapter 16). We are instructed to "Believe in the complete and return to it" (chapter 22). Both a return to "infancy" and a return to "limitlessness" supposedly result from a true understanding of the perfection of the Tao (chapter 28). "Return" is considered to be the "motion" of the Tao, because the Tao takes all things and "returns" them to

their source, even as it gives birth to them. This can be thought of as one motion, not as two distinct forces of creation and re-traction; being born is not only a condition of dying—birth guar-antees death. Likewise, "softening" is an important aspect of the Tao that can be thought of in relation to life and death. Since the Tao is yielding and is not differentiated, it can be said to unify in itself the creative processes of life-giving and the weakening and decaying processes of mortality. "All things submit to *yin* and em-brace *yang*. / They soften their energy to achieve harmony" (chapter 42).

22. (chapter 42) *I regard this as the father of all teachings*: This is the only reference to the "father" in the *Tao Te Ching*. The source of all things (as opposed to one particular teaching, as here) is usu-ally called the "mother" and identified with the Tao itself.

23. (chapter 43) *unattached action*: The Chinese term for this concept is *wu-wei*.

24. (chapter 45) *Excitement overcomes cold, stillness overcomes heat*: There is some disagreement on how this line should be trans-lated and understood. Some commentators think that the text should be read literally, in which case "excitement" and "still-ness" are to be considered as stronger forces than "cold" and "heat." But others think that this does not make sense, given that the Tao is understood primarily in terms of the reconciliation of opposites. Opposite forces do not overcome each other in the sense of confronting and warring against each other, but rather overcome each other in the way that one wave overcomes an-other. In other words, they follow naturally from each other: Cool motionlessness leads to excitement and energy, and heated agitation is followed by periods of calm. "Clarity and stillness" together refer to the kind of harmony and equilibrium associated with the Tao, in which disparate principles balance one another naturally and spontaneously.

25. (chapter 49) *The sages treat them as their little children*: The image of infancy here is probably not meant to suggest paternalistic

government, but rather government that is in harmony with the natural innocence of unspoiled people.

26. (chapter 50) *Because he has no death-ground*: To have "no death-ground" might mean to have no body, or to have transcended identification with one's mortal body.

27. (chapter 52) *Stop up the holes / Shut the doors*: The holes and doors of the self are its eyes, nose, mouth, and ears, those sensory organs that "open" the mind to the external world.

28. (chapter 55) *One who remains rich in virtuous power / Is like a newborn baby*: The newborn is a symbol of the Tao: helpless, uncultivated, unspoiled, natural, and innocent. Its mind can be compared to an uncarved block—empty of any of the conceptual distinctions of language. It is pure because it follows completely its intuition and natural perceptions. Because it is so weak, it is not aggressive toward anything else in the world and, in turn, nothing attacks it. In contrast, that which "blossoms" and develops into a distinct form is closer to dying. Things that strive to establish their own natures apart from natural spontaneity are thus "non-Tao."

29. (chapter 55) *Having control of your breath is called strength*: This may be a reference to Taoist yogic practices, in which techniques of breath control were used to nourish the energy of the body.

30. (chapter 60) *Ruling a large country is like cooking a small fish*: Small fish can be damaged by being handled too much or too roughly.

31. (chapter 63) *Respond to anger with virtue*: This teaching is found in many religious and ethical traditions. In the context of Taoism, the injunction to "respond to anger with virtue" has a distinct justification. One is to respond to the anger, injury, or hatred of another with compassion, but not because this would make one into a more virtuous person who will be judged more favorably by a moral authority. Rather, one does this because one understands the nature of the Tao as undifferentiated and without a moral hierarchy. To blame or justify retaliation on the basis of another's wrongdoing would be to see wrong and right as opposites of one

another, not as relative distinctions that dissolve in the unity of the Tao.

32. (chapter 69) *The one who is sorry about it will be the winner*: The claim that "the one who is sorry about [a fight] will be the winner" can be interpreted in various ways. The passage might simply be pointing out that one who regrets engaging with violence because it leads to destruction and enmity is the wiser for being aware of this. But how does simply being more prudent make one "the winner"? Feeling sorry about a clash might also entail entering it reluctantly and being prepared to lose. From a Taoist perspective, it is this very humility and lack of aggression that will preserve one's life. As discussed in note 18, "Victory is never sweet." One who desires victory over others perpetuates a cycle of resistance and violence that can only decrease one's likelihood of survival.

33. (chapter 77) *The Way of Heaven / Is like stretching a bow*: One stretches a bow to test it and make any needed adjustments.

34. (chapter 80) *Let them return to measurement by tying knots in rope*: "Tying knots in rope" is a very simple way of doing measurements and calculations, one that is less sophisticated than the method in use when this passage was written.

For Further Reading

OTHER EDITIONS OF THE TAO TE CHING

The following are widely considered to be reliable, readable translations of the Tao Te Ching, *accompanied by textual notes.*

Chen, Ellen M., trans. *The Tao Te Ching: A New Translation with Commentary.* New York: Paragon House, 1989. Informative and detailed commentary on each chapter.

Feng, Gia-Fu, and Jane English, trans. *Lao Tsu: Tao Te Ching.* New York: Alfred A. Knopf, 1972.

Henricks, Robert G., trans. *Lao-tzu: Te-Tao Ching.* New York: Ballantine Books, 1989.

Lau, D. C., trans. *Lao Tzu: Tao Te Ching.* Baltimore: Penguin, 1963. A particularly fine translation, with a very thorough introductory discussion.

Mair, Victor H., trans. *Tao Te Ching: The Classic Book of Integrity and the Way.* New York: Bantam Books, 1990.

TAOISM

Cleary, Thomas F. *Immortal Sisters: Secrets of Taoist Women.* Boston: Shambhala, 1989. A history of the role of women in Taoism, a topic that is not often covered in other discussions.

Creel, Herrlee G. *What Is Taoism? And Other Studies in Chinese Cultural History.* Chicago: University of Chicago Press, 1970. Contains some important introductory essays, including the title one.

Csikszentmihalyi, Mark, and Philip J. Ivanhoe, eds. *Religious and Philosophical Aspects of the Laozi.* Albany: State University of New York Press, 1999. A recent set of essays from scholars of Lao Tzu; for the more advanced reader.

Hansen, Chad. *A Daoist Theory of Chinese Thought: A Philosophical Interpretation*. New York: Oxford University Press, 1992. A more philosophical approach to Taoism, examining its role in the context of disputes between various schools of thought.

Kohn, Livia, ed. *The Taoist Experience: An Anthology*. Albany: State University of New York Press, 1993. An anthology containing readings from a wide variety of Taoist texts.

————, ed. *Taoist Meditation and Longevity Techniques*. Ann Arbor: Center for Chinese Studies, University of Michigan, 1989. For those who wish to learn more about Taoist yogic practices and associated beliefs.

Kohn, Livia, and Michael LaFargue, eds. *Lao-Tzu and the Tao-Te-Ching*. Albany: State University of New York Press, 1998. A recent collection of interpretative essays by scholars of the *Tao Te Ching*.

Li Po and Tu Fu. *Bright Moon, Perching Bird*. Translated by J. P. Seaton and James Cryer. Middletown, CT: Wesleyan University Press, 1987. A collection of Taoist poetry for those interested in the literary aspect of Taoism.

Mair, Victor H., trans. *Wandering on the Way: Early Taoist Tales and Parables of Chuang Tzu*. Honolulu: University of Hawaii Press, 1998. A recent translation of the works of Lao Tzu's successor; the introduction includes a concise summary of early Chinese thought.

Merton, Thomas. *Chuang Tzu: The Way of Chuang Tzu*. New York: New Directions, 1965. A mystic perspective on Taoism. Working from four existing translations, Merton, a Roman Catholic monk, composed personal versions from his favorites among Chuang Tzu's sayings.

Watson, Burton, trans. *Chuang Tzu: Basic Writings*. New York: Columbia University Press, 1964. Considered to be a poetic, lyrical translation of the main works of Chuang Tzu.

————, trans. *The Complete Works of Chuang Tzu*. New York: Columbia University Press, 1968.

ANCIENT CHINESE PHILOSOPHY

De Bary, William Theodore, and Irene Bloom, eds. *Sources of Chinese Tradition*. New York: Columbia University Press, 1999. A fine anthology with good introductions to the various key selections; suitable for beginning students.

Graham, Angus C. *Disputers of the Tao: Philosophical Argument in Ancient China*. La Salle, IL: Open Court, 1989. An excellent general history of ancient Chinese philosophy, introducing the reader to the various schools of thought.

Ivanhoe, Philip J., and Bryan W. Van Norden, eds. *Readings in Classical Chinese Philosophy*. New York and London: Seven Bridges Press, 2001. A comprehensive anthology featuring key excerpts from early Chinese texts with very fine contemporary translations.

Lau, D. C. *Confucius: The Analects*. Harmondsworth and New York: Penguin Books, 1979. One of the most widely used translations of this central Confucian text, with a very good introduction and various appendices.

Legge, James. *Confucian Analects, the Great Learning, and the Doctrine of the Mean*. New York: Dover Books, 1971. An older translation (the original printing dates to 1893), but it includes the two most important Confucian texts apart from the *Analects*. In addition to detailed textual notes, this volume includes a useful dictionary of characters.

Munro, Donald J. *The Concept of Man in Early China*. Stanford, CA: Stanford University Press, 1969. A comparison of Confucian and Taoist views, as well as comparison of both with the Western tradition.

Schwartz, Benjamin I. *The World of Thought in Ancient China*. Cambridge, MA: Belknap Press, 1985. Like Graham's *Disputers of the Tao* (see above), considered to be an outstanding general history.